Books by Charlotte Brady

Och den fula ängelen föll

Villfarelser

Detaljernas tämjare

The Golden Passage Trilogy

As Silence Is Your Witness

Midnight Transit

The Last Star

The Last Star

THE LAST STAR

Poems

Charlotte Brady

ANTERIOR BOOKS

THE LAST STAR. Copyright © 2017 by Charlotte Brady.

All rights reserved. This book, or parts thereof, may not be reproduced in any form without the express written permission of the publisher. Printed in the United States of America.

ISBN-13: 978-0-9976182-2-8
ISBN-10: 0997618221

Anterior Books
P.O. Box 832469
Miami, FL 33283
www.anterior.us

Cover design by Ingenious Tek Group

First Printing

(Prologue)

A Star

Perhaps I will become a speck of dust. Perhaps I will be happy without memories. Perhaps I will be drunk on the promised wine. Perhaps I will still be thirsty. Perhaps I will be nothing. When I woke up I remembered a single dream. You kept me in a jar; I was your last experiment. I invited strangers and offered them your wine. Most of them declined. Let there be love, you said. I smiled. I am a master of nothing. I cling to no thing, deeply rooted in a star.

Next Morning

Good morning, world. You swallowed me whole and I ate you in return. Now we'll be burping together until midday. After that, we'll see—
I stayed eaten several hours, aimlessly wandering in your garden. Then you threw me up. What disgrace! Wallowing in your vomit, I tried to understand what happened. I still had your density planted in my flesh and I was marked by gravity. Wine bottle in hand, I kept knocking on your door but you never opened. Hence I went to bed, knowing you'd swallow me whole again next morning.

For What?

I don't know if the world

stopped making sense to me

or if I stopped making sense to the world.

Either way we are damned.

This heart,

this one heart,

ripped out and crushed.

This heart,

this one heart,

denied and betrayed.

This holy heart.

This divine gift we share. For what?

A Dream

The moment my solitude turns into loneliness, I reach out into space. I take what is not there and comfort my hungry soul. The soul doesn't understand yet that solitude is a home. It can't detect the exact moment it falls out of its nest; it can't prevent itself from falling. It can't perceive the border. It can't understand the transition into pain. By then it's too late and the soul believes it's hungry again. It doesn't understand yet that loneliness has faded into a dream.

No Ending

Decondition yourself. Dismember memories. The past carries no truth. Begin again. Invite the present and then let it drop, again and again. Walk blindly into the day. It won't leave traces if you leave it alone. Your skin is just a suggestion. It's not where you end. For you there is no ending.

Dumbfounded Me

A fountain wells up inside. It spreads its waters everywhere. I am the water and you are the water. Ah, bliss. The nature of what we are: the spraying of the ocean, dew drops on tall grass, rain on ripened fruit, love's simple communion. Oh, love, bliss is yours and yours is bliss. Oh, love, the beginning and dissolution of everything. Oh, love, the fountain in our hearts that never dries. Oh, bliss—blah, blah, bliss. There is more to be found than you.

In Me

This sacred room has no walls. It feels like loneliness at first. But we all share the same universe. In seconds we are transported into space. Stars are strewn over our bodies. Miracles happen every instant. All relationships have lost their meaning. At first we are afraid because relationship is all we know. Then we understand and disappear into one another. My heart is yours. Your heart silently beats in me.

Infinite Peace

There is much to learn from a tree's silence. How it holds its branches in peace. How its thoughts only briefly touch the leaves. There is much to learn about its stillness. Year after year it stays in one place. It never gets tired of where it is. It never dreams of something else. It is first to greet the sun and last to watch the moon pale into another day. In darkness the roots grow and in secret seeds develop. If you stay close to a tree, you will hear it talk. It wants to hold you, like its branches are held, in infinite peace.

Too Late

Incorporating evil, chewing it. Opening up to its essence and there: love is found. Evil is not separate from good. Choose the right angle. Someone will always accuse you of being evil. Someone will always accuse you of being good. Don't fight it. Don't run away from it. Eat it up. Make yourself bigger, rise into the sky. Swallow more and more of the eternal blue. Become softer and harder, sober and drunk. This is how you attack your enemy. Only you can turn evil into love, only you. I accuse you of being that which you already are. Now remember it. Then nothing is too late.

Future Gardening

Being arrogant and mean, I am watching the night sky. There is plenty darkness. Wanting to receive but not to give, I close my hands. My heart is empty. It reflects the sky. A moon would pull the strings and release the clinging, open eyes and plant some stars for future gardening.

Ending Here

If I were enlightened, I would not write a poem about evil. Wait! I got it backwards—the right way to read it is l-i-v-e. I have to stop living backwards and see the truth. Don't forget to breathe. Dreams live in the womb until they are born. Remember to wink once you know. Walk straight. Go on, go on. There is no ending here.

Imagined Life

A silver arrow in the sunset. People coming and going. Young love has many wings. How can something so elusive ever be lost? We sow seeds and reap what we think. My heart belongs to the sky. The unknown is larger than this imagined life.

A Thing

Things drop away. Like unintended gestures they fade from Earth. "What remains?" you may ask. That remains. That—indefinite. You think you are running towards something but you are running away, losing all you dream of. You think you are gaining but you are losing. Garments fall off my body. What silly decorations. How dysfunctional. I stand naked and nobody can see me. To some, only my discards are visible. To some, my freedom is revolting. I haven't lost a thing.

All Begins

The universe follows you everywhere you go.
Like a shadow it's attached to your very being.
You turn to it for answers, you question it,
you fight it, despise it; a windmill in your dream.
Until all means are exhausted, so it goes.
This is not your game; you are being played.
And there is nothing you can do about it.
This is where you meet yourself, in glory
dirtied by your hopes. This is where it all begins.

A Mouth

I am a recluse and a social butterfly, a bud in full flowering, a tree inside a seed. I go here and there in silence. Turmoil breaks a nail. Ouch! My wings are thin but steady. Why should I even speak? I don't have a mouth.

Isn't Much

You collect things, experiences, memories, and knowledge. What for? None of this you may keep. Everything must go. So insanely happy over nothing. So joyous for all my losses. What was worth keeping? Nothing, I'd say. Nothing is worth keeping. Compared to everything, nothing isn't much.

Somewhere Else

I saw I was a dream. You looked at me and saw a tree. I put my hand right through you, and you survived long enough to know you also wanted to reach the other shore. I won't carry my boat or tie it up. I'll send it back for when you're thirsty, for when you're ready to drink the whole ocean to find that single drop. The journey is long, but what do you have but time? Time is all you have. All you know is time. Time is what you think you are, time in all dimensions. Meet me somewhere else.

That Love

This is a love that never dies. This is a love that was never born. This is a love that sees. This is a love that is free. This is a love that has no need to know. This is a love that will neither expand nor diminish. This is a love that is. This is a love that never desires. This is a love that asks for nothing. This is a love that reaches your darkest place. This is a love that stops for nothing. This is a love from which nothing can hide. This is a love that is silent. This is a love that keeps moving through rock. This is a love that warms what was frozen. This is. That love.

A Snake

I killed a snake by accident. I saw it writhe in agony. It wasn't a rope. It was a snake. It was real. I am real. My regret is real. How I wish the rope was in the snake but this snake was nothing but a snake.

I Go

This poem is all I am. Yet I am not this poem. This heart is all I know. Yet I don't know this heart. This Earth is all we have. Yet we don't have this Earth. The sun and the moon, the trees and the rain, they come and go and I go, I go. I go and I go.

This Painting

I hurl wild brushstrokes in a heart. The line moves while failing to grasp the ungraspable picture of life. What is a rock? What is a tree? What is their source and meaning? The brushstroke outlines form and penetrates an unseen core. I hold reality in the palm of my hand. Eternity melts and blends with the motif. We are invisible inside this painting.

Love's Touch

You once were a dream I had. Then I stopped dreaming and you were gone. I don't want you back because you weren't real. I just thought you were. Not even my dream was real; it was dreamed within a dream. Nothing is holy—holiness *is*. Your face, divinity's mirror. Your hands, love's touch.

For You

I return each word to its silence, each meaning to its source, until there is only my breath, my heartbeat, my pulsation, in the entire universe. Such is the love I am for you.

The Abyss

Early morning, sitting like a Buddha in your red bathrobe. Hands on your lap and a wine glass full of rum, as if meditating on the nature of intoxication. I pass by, shake my head and go to bed again. I want to say, "Father, don't let go of the railing," but I say nothing. I don't live here anymore. Afterwards I say to myself, "It was already too late. He had already let go with one hand. He was already dangling over the abyss."

An Essence

Father, for eighty years you carried this body. Now it's gone, gone for good. Your bones are burned and your thoughts are secret. For eighty years your body was subject to change. You had many names. What are you now? "Dead" is not an attribute, nor an essence.

Was Possible

The old streets will never carry your footsteps. The lost neighborhoods will never come alive again. There will be no glimpse of you walking out of a photograph. No glimpse of who you really were. What you could have been. What I could have been. What we could have had. The sky in those old photographs is always very close and dry. Silent, as a reflection of the words we never said. The houses are empty, from a time when everything still was possible.

Delicious Cake

You can't express yourself through a human body anymore. You have stopped creating dreams. You will never have another discussion about earthly matters. You will not smoke or drink, think or feel. You won't see the sun rise through the body's eyes again. You will never choose to catch that fish, nor choose to let it go. Your body has ceased to function, the clock stopped ticking. Where are you now and what "you" am I referring to? How could you stop being in existence? Or did you just move on to have a different slice of this delicious cake?

You Understand

I don't miss what we had as much as what we could have had. Instead of closeness we had approximations and misunderstandings. Instead of joy we had habits and scripts. But there was love, still. Even though we didn't know it. Or maybe we did? You know me more intimately in death than you did in life. You hear me now and you are not afraid. Now—you understand.

I Know

Blinking stars far away, a cry for help. Light extinguished a long time ago, light extinguished now, light still glowing. The lonely souls departed, where are they now? Life goes on, light goes on, shining after darkness. Twinkle, star. Twinkle now. What you are, I know.

Another Birth

The depth of our insignificance is astonishing. Little specks of light are lit and then blown out by an unexpected breeze. "Look at me, I blink." "Look at me, my light is dimmed." "Look at me, I shine." "Look at me, I'm going into darkness." Countless lights are lit, extinguished day by day. For a while each light lives on inside other lights, but eventually they all go back into the source of light, into the darkness that gives birth to hope and hope to another birth.

In Rain

The red cardinal hides from the rain. It sits in the fig tree under an umbrella leaf. The water is pouring like I'm pouring myself into nature. I am nowhere to be found. The red cardinal flies off and finds his friend. I find myself and dissolve in rain.

I Forgot

First I relax. Then I do nothing. Then I relax again. A lot of people do something. I do nothing. Later I talk to my friend about doing nothing.

The clouds are passing. We count them. We arrive at the same number. Then we count again and arrive at a different number. The sun is warm today. The leaves are dancing. How many clouds did we find? I forgot.

Of Gold

Look into your heart's mirror and see how free you are, how beautiful. Don't look away. Look closer and closer. Never once look outside. The world is telling you that you are ugly, but your heart knows you are beautiful. Don't listen to malevolent voices. Here, you can be at peace. Here, you are the ruler. Remember not to beg for poverty. Your begging bowl was made of gold.

Hear Them

There is no up or down, east or west. There are no compasses that work over here. There is no forward, no backward. Even love is an illusion, perhaps the last. There is nothing to hope for and nothing you have to do. Here, love and hope are spells you seek to break. These are the forbidden words. This is the secret that should remain untold. Do not say it or you'll be thrown out of paradise. Mouths that can form these words do not exist, nor do ears that want to hear them.

Your Hair

I am free like the wind. Nothing can define me. I occupy any space. I dance through leaves and take charge of hollowness. My changelessness shapes itself into any form. Nothing can touch me, nothing can move me. I am touch. I am movement. Think of me when the wind kisses your shoulder. Think of me when the wind plays with your hair.

Being Love

Lots of struggle. Heavy. No restraint applied. Walking through thorny woods. No judgment of judgment. No indictment. Meeting myself in seedy shadows. Head on. Being with myself.
Being myself. Being. Love.

Abandoned Hearts

I hold you in my heart. Nothing bad can happen. My love is a blanket, a starry night sky. It keeps you warm and safe. Relax into the shape of a sleeping infant. Relax. No fight, no struggle. No running, no escaping. You are here with me. I hold you. For once, stay with me—stay. For your own sake—stay with yourself. Don't be frightened. Let's meet in our abandoned hearts.

Your Skin

The cosmology of your heart is a labyrinth. To find yourself, listen intently to birds singing or the yawning of a dog. Find yourself in the movement of a snail, the opening of a seed, the scent trail of an ant. That movement is you, that existence. That is where you will find yourself after looking so long, after crying countless nights: you are right there, right here, in you, in me. Inside that memory, which is an echo of something so distant that it is closer than your skin.

Another Here

The day was like a postcard with a beautiful motif. The moments had no boundaries, each floated into the other. Lavishly, free. The card contained every corner of the world but undelivered, sender unknown, stamp torn. The day gone, another here.

Not Here

I will disappear until there is no trace of me. First I fell into a lake of ecstasy, then sucked out into a river of joy and washed out into the ocean. I'm currently nowhere but also everywhere—
a droplet merging. Adjectives are useless in describing me. I am not no one. I am not someone. I am so not here.

Not There

Waiting for the rainwater to settle and reflect my face. I sing a new song to the moon. It's a song I can't teach you. You are fighting a phantom and refuse to look at me. There is nothing I can do to make you see me. You are so not there.

Your Tempest

I am caught in a rainfall. If I engage it goes on. If I disengage it goes on. I watch the rain soak my clothes. The sun smiles behind the clouds and you suffer in your tempest.

Maybe Not

What does it matter if someone tries to hurt me from the well of their sorrow? They are not home and there is nothing I can do. I will let them hurt me until they are tired. They will tire before I am hurt because there is no one here to wound. I am the sky, the mountains, and the rivers. I am the birds, the sun, and the stars. When they have exhausted all their bitterness but still unsatisfied, I will speak. Maybe they will hear me. Maybe not.

Myself Rich

Oh, how I love to be with myself and spend time in the garden of faith. I pick flowers and roll in the grass. I run with my arms stretched towards the sun. I have everything I need. I am me. I live in a moment that never ends and now is all I have. I never feel lonely. My lovely friends are with me. The ants, the lizards, the butterflies. I count them all and consider myself rich.

Had It

You ask me for help but don't want to hear what I'm saying. You want me to say certain words but I can only say the wordless. You can't remember me, or you don't know that I exist. I'm not a magician. You think you are helpless but you are a god. You think I'm different but we are the same. Every day you beg while walking by my side. You keep asking for help and I breathe for you. It's not my answer you are begging for. You want your heart back but I never had it.

Already Free

Meeting a dead sage, I said: I hope you can see straight through me. I hope your gaze will burn everything I think I am. I hope there will be nothing left of me but ashes and then I hope you will burn those, too. I hope to know that I do not know. I hope to be free of what I think I know. The sage looked at me and said: I already know you. I don't even have to look. You are already free.

Practice

Yesterday was the most successful day of my life and today is my first day of practice after twenty-five years of practice. I was the sun firmly placed in the sky. I was the moon's reflection. I was the sea reaching the shore. I was the bird flying south. For twenty-five years I practiced to be able to practice. Tomorrow will be my first day of practice.

Day Out

With each inhale, practice living. With each exhale, practice dying. While awake, practice being. While asleep, practice non-being. Passively contemplate, actively practice. Day in, day out.

Practice This

Eating your words, I glow. Calling out your name, I am your tongue. Breathing your essence, I am air. You told me: One Whole Day of Continuous Practice Is a Bright Jewel. You told me to keep replacing the way with the way with the way. This word is the continuous practice: this.

Empty

Coffee and a blow to the head. The past dissolving into that coffee. No teacher, no student. That coffee taking on the shape of the past, the past only existing in that cup of coffee. The smell of coffee in the house, the blow to the head, the smell in the head. Where is the mother and the father? Where is the child? Now drink that coffee and tell me where the past is when that cup is empty.

Our Origin

Millions and millions have emerged from nothing and then succumbed to nothing. I emerged and will soon succumb. You emerged and will also soon succumb. What we do between these points of nothing is valueless as long as we refuse to know ourselves. We try to look away from nothingness by acquiring for the moment. But nothingness is the only thing you truly own. We are running away from our eternity. Nothingness is beautiful. Nothingness is our origin.

Be Silent

To talk about these matters is insane. Keep to yourself and breathe. Remember your spine at all times and the well at the bottom of your eyes, the place you come from. Hold others' hands and be quiet but beyond all—be silent.

But Love

Every cell in me contemplates existence. Every star does, too. We blink to one another because we know who we are. Blink—I'm here. Blink—I'm gone. If we knew our privilege of being, there would be nothing left but love.

Are Alive

We are far behind with everything, even ourselves. We chose loving over living right. I've been clueless for the most part of my time on this planet, and I believe everyone else has too. Life is not a standardized test. You won't know until it's too late. No alternatives are given. We are far behind with everything. I might call this experimentation a failure because failures are alive.

Becomes Full

When you are without memory of how love should be, the word love loses its meaning and becomes being. The word becomes empty and your being becomes full.

To Fly

Mother, you have become a little bird. Your body shivers from not remembering. I tell you the same joke a million times and you laugh as if it were funny, as if life were begging you to stay alive. I love how you became bohemian with age. You didn't care as much, you started laughing more, forgetting more about the darkness. Your wings are flapping and I know you will soon remember how to fly.

You Listen

I was already here. I was the sound before it started sounding. I was the light before the darkness. I am not becoming or evolving. I am the suffering you endure. I am the nail forced into your body. I am your desperation, your inability to protect everything you love. I am your powerlessness. I am the beliefs that proved worthless in the end. I hold you while you are dying. I am born when you give birth. I am the love that is never seen but always there. Never lost. Never gone. Never silent if you listen.

Or Fly

Last night I gave birth to you a second time. I was afraid of my own shadow and so you couldn't be fully born. Some parts stayed in me. I let them go. You are free to walk, or fly.

Well Rested

No. I rest in no other rest. No. Problems are created. Let them uncreate themselves. It's in their nature to dissolve into no. No is not negating. No is not. No other love. No other God. No face. No trace. I see you clearly because you gave me your eyes. I woke up from sleep and felt well rested.

A Void

I have everything and everything is lacking.

I have seen everything and I have never seen it.

I am a stranger and a friend, a heart and a brain.

I am a breath and a heartbeat, a star and a void.

Am Alive

I am as grateful as a tree. Standing tall and firm, roots in the ground, going deeper. Crown in the sky, going higher. My branches are a resting place for birds. In the rain I give shelter. In the sun I give shade. My limbs are made for swings. I extend my arms to embrace the universe. In the night my leaves go black against the night sky. I am still. I breathe in silence. I am alive.

The Clouds

Tearful joy. Prayerful love. Distant past. Present now. Joyful sorrow in plain sight. Valleys, peaks, and rivers. I follow you. Your steps are in the clouds.

To Learn

Did the stars get caught up in fighting today? Did they get stuck in orbit? Was there some glitch in the machinery, a crack in the illusion? A certain restlessness from God? Imagine his distress. Humankind has not evolved since creation. How sad. We never seem to learn.

For You

All the cells are aflame in my body. The fire is spreading to my heart. My head is wide open. The descent has begun. Or ascent. It doesn't matter. Direction has no meaning. I am, dear one, I am. I am another name for you.

It All

I am available for the universe. I am its home. When you die, the world's fights will still be fought. Even your own fight will be carried on, in the shape of others. It's the meaning of endlessness. But that is not what I mean by that word. I mean love when I say endlessness. I mean the perfect gaze into your eyes that say it all.

Of Blood

My friend, my heart beats in your hand. Take care. Be soft even if you don't know how. Be gentle as if holding a newborn. I am a newborn. I am born to myself every day. You are there with me. Let the endless fights run out. Let them quieten down, become silent like leaves on a windless night. Just know your pain. It's all you have to do. Know your pain and see it. That is all. It's when you run away that you start to fight. It's in your endless running that you smell of blood.

I Die

If you don't like my poems, you can address that with their source. I have nothing to do with their production. I simply move my fingers and a poem is born. How surprised I am to see their spirit. I look into their eyes. I will never understand their mystery. Never know their source. I will care for them until I die.

Longing Possibility

Today I was told a secret: this tree is in love with you. It has dreamed of you since time began. The roots go as deep as its love. The branches reach the sky in laughter. This tree is joyful because you exist. It grows leaves only for you. It wants you to hear every single leaf sigh of sweet longing for your touch. It wants you to smile the way you smile when you are completely unafraid. It wants you to rest in its shade. This tree teaches birds their love songs every spring. It wants you to hear them sing. They sing about the love this tree feels for you. They sing about longing, possibility.

Your Existence

Take my words if you like. Crumble them up into tiny pieces and spread them for the wind. Let them become unspoken, unwritten, understood only by microscopic organisms. Let them fly like butterflies and die a butterfly's death, unknown and forgotten. Take my words and let them drown in lovers' kisses or burn in their passion. Let them fade in the morning sky and disappear that way forever. Or if you don't want my words: speak them for me. Write them in your handwriting and let me be lost in your experience.

Empty Words

When you drop all the faces you thought were you, bliss arrives in a shiny car to pick you up. You are going for a ride. A long ride. It will never end. Now you don't care about any of your faces. You don't care what face others see in you or what name they give you. None of it has meaning. All this time you thought you had to succeed and fix. All this time you thought you were different. Hilarious! Now you're having a party with the universe. You dance and twirl. You are dizzy and shameless in your freedom. Joy! Bliss! They are not empty words.

Ultimate Creation

Lust runs through the body. I am empty and wish to be filled up. I embrace you in my universe. Not withholding, giving everything. This is the entry to your desire, gravity will pull you in. My innocence is greater than the sky. I own you now like I own myself. We are one in longing. You are relentless but I surround you. Waves wash over your identity. Dissolve in me, I beg. The sea meets the tide, as it always has. The motion goes on forever; the rhythm of the universe; life's beginning; mystery of mysteries; echoes of the ultimate creation.

Wanting More

Who dares to hold my love? Who is capable of receiving? Who is ready to give up longing? My love is patient, never in a hurry. It's not going anywhere. Perhaps you forgot yourself. Perhaps you got afraid of drowning. Love is here—now. Love is oxygen. If you drink it, it will never run out. If you eat it, you won't feel hunger again. Who dares to give up hunger for good? Who dares to give up the pleasure of wanting more?

I Am

Today the moon followed me on my morning walk, a pearl hanging in the sky showering love over my bewildered path. It showed no sign of hurry to set before the sun rose, elegantly balancing night and day in my miniature steps. As if trying to determine who I am.

Out There

The Immense Sorrow of Humankind and Its Immanent Solution: The way out is the way in. The way out is the way through. The way out is the way beyond. The way out is the way. The way out is. The way. Way, way out. There.

Will Crumble

I wish I could breathe love into people's hearts. True love, not just a proclamation. I wish I could sprinkle seeds of compassion. True compassion, not just convenience. I wish I could whisper the meaning of a life's worth in ears that lost their hearing. I wish I could send protection to those defenseless. A heart against a knife. An embrace against a missile. Love's power speaks quietly.
In the end all your weapons shall turn against you and hate will crumble.

You Are

Everythingness, I am in love! I want you for who you are.

Origin Love

My face in all the faces, yet I am nowhere to be found. An echo of infinity—I fall into myself. This is what I term my birth, the body's birth. I return this machine to eternity once its duty on Earth is over. With every heartbeat a little of the finite is exhausted. With every touch I am reminded of my origin, love.

In Time

When I walk, the universe follows me like a comet's tail. I'm the poet in the landscape, which is urban and pristine. When dust reflects sunlight, it's a thing. Yet I am nothing, a no-thing. Don't make me into a thing. I am not a mask and nothing can define me. I have no traits, no history, and no belongings. The whole world is mine or nothing is. This is where I exist. In my own landscape. I have no qualities. I am the landscape, winding between cars and highways, happy, free, in time.

Intimately Free

Crow crowing in the distance. Dog sniffing. Who is walking? All is well, I remember. The presence of other birds, lesser known. The presence of life, intimately free.

Constant Imitation

I am an amateur. Let me never be an expert. No darkness in my eyes, only open doors. You can enter at any time but there is fear. Fearlessness is far away but near. Sometimes you try, then you forget. Then you remember, then you regret. I am a lover. I can never teach. There is only intimation of the truth and you reach it by constant imitation.

Saw It

Today I saw the last star, but it disappeared behind some trees before I got a chance to watch it fade into nonexistence. It fizzled in a pink and lazy morning sky, a bright white speck—the last illusion. Cars before me, cars behind—morning rush. The star showed itself reluctantly. I will have to beg to see it again. Or fully forget I ever saw it.

There Arrived

What is fear from this side of eternity? It is still nothing. Caught in the spiderweb of mind. What is the spider? You are lucky to return. Try one more time and you'll be gone. Fear made you into a person. I have forgotten why that once seemed attractive. I dwindle now and skip the rest.

Fast forward, rewind, and pause. There, arrived.

It Stops

Looking at the last star before the day breaks into light. The last star and this moment seem to be extended into forever. I am here. I have traveled to this place and I have arrived completely, as I am. Many traveled with me. They held my hand. They carried me. The sounds of their whispering voices are still with me. All of us under one sky, one sun, one moon. Luckily there is no fighting for this. In this region there is no point in fighting. Everybody sees it and it stops.

Mistaken Understanding

I couldn't understand that there was nothing to understand. What comes in this manner? Nothing comes in this manner. A body comes and goes, but nothing comes and nothing goes. Is it that? The mind fought to stay on top by its desire to understand. It won because it seemed so reasonable. Then there were many years of apparent insanity.

Tears

When the heart cries, the stars fade a tiny bit. When the ache inside the chest is unbearable, the moon starts singing. The comfort is for those in need. The need is endless because we can't forget our flesh. Teaching history will only aggravate the situation. Leaving us alone is useless since we will find a way to dream our sorrow back again. Listen to the moon's delicate song tonight. It sings for you. Soon the stars will brighten up again and cause the heart to dry its tears.

Call Love

Soon I am wiped out. Soon I am empty space. Like the chrysanthemum is a placeholder for nothingness, I am too. Soon my only home is in someone's memory. Soon I am a number without measuring anything. Soon I am someone's breath. If they count me, they will wake up and remember who I am. One, one, one. Welcome to eternity, I'll say when they wake up. Then fear shall turn into what they call love.

Losing Everything

After fear love is. When fear is made invisible, you stumble on a rock at night. You hurt. Someone hurts. You hurt. All activities are toys to keep fear at bay. Fear will make you helpless, as helpless as you are. As helpless as you don't want to be. Beyond fear is love. There is no way except through fear and willingness to losing everything.

Turn White

Who is looking at me? Someone who has looked at me for a million years with the same freaking gaze. Someone who has adored me unceasingly for eons. Who is looking at me? Is it an eye looking into an eye? Or an I looking into itself? Is it nobody looking into nothing? Who is looking and what do they see and what is the purpose of all this looking? I will ask the baby ibis birds, before their feathers all turn white.

The Unborn

Happy birthday to you, today! You carry your meaning for a lifetime and give birth to yourself. The meaning is ingrained in your flesh and in your thoughts, a tiny reflection of your originality. Your importance is indisputable. You are the meaning of life. Now nurture the unborn.

Mother's Breast

Live at the border of the unknown. Let it move into you. Allow it to create a habitat in your heart. Live by it. Drown in it. Drink it. Be like an infant at the Mother's breast.

I Know

A flower smiled at me today and told me I am beautiful. She also told me that everything I know is false. A flower told it to me. Now, that is the only thing I know.

As You

When all desires become irrelevant, I bow my head which is no longer a head but a heart that I place in your hands. You loved me all this time as yourself. As yourself you saw me in the distance. The leaves of the star apple tree move shiny and deep into the light wind. Now this is who I am; a movement in the atmosphere. So near that everything is revealed as you, me, us.

By One

When I was looking out the window, a downy feather fell through the air. Then all was still again as if that weightlessness had never happened. It fell silently like the snowflakes of childhood, the ones we caught on our tongues and melted in the fire of our breath. While playing in the snow, night came and stars were watching as we grew older one by one.

Heal You

Unknowingly I burned a hole for love to enter. My temporary face does not look like my original face. I have aged but not changed. My skin against yours for eons. Do you remember me? Answer, because time won't wait for you.

It's already too late, don't let it go to waste. The world is burning and you are fighting the wrong fire. Let it burn a hole in you. Don't be afraid of love. It will hurt but trust will heal you.

In Flames

In silent ecstasy I am breathing you. No more names. No more past. Live with me here. What is eternal in you is eternal in me. We share the same blood. Our origin is identical. Remember your past in such a way that it becomes your heart, then let it burn, disappear in flames.

Embarrassing Mortality

If we could remember this moment at the time of our birth, it would never go as wrong as it always does. Every second would be stopped and held accountable. Every breath would be meaningful and important. Peace would reign and love would be our fate. If we could remember this moment before it is too late, we would be saved from this embarrassing mortality.

For Celebration

On New Year's Eve the skeletons are dancing in the hall. There's smoke and mirrors, fur and lipstick. They do that every year. They do what they can to stay happy with themselves. They put their makeup on, fighting distant shadows. Nothing matters anymore but they go on polishing their bones, putting on perfume and silk scarves, forgetting that death is already their reality, believing rotting flesh might be a cause for celebration.

Consciousness Again

My heart was made hollow to make room for your love. Still inside my chest, beating softly, the emptiness of it frightened me. The sun between the leaves, like stars, mistaken identities. I for one fell hard and long into my shadow. I only now start gaining consciousness again.

I Survived

Pregnant with eternity, round like the Earth. Full of everything and nothing, I walk these streets carrying this instant in me. I am happy now, and now. Past actions are gone, new ones not initiated. There is nothing to wait for and nothing to long for. Nothing to resent. Nothing to regret. Nothing to fear. A new birth is here. I discovered I am the world. I gave birth and I succumbed. I died and I survived.

Puppy Heart

Renouncing a dream of love I became love.

There is no difference between a bird and myself, between a worm and myself. The bird eats the worm and flies into the sky. End of story. The seeds are stars sprinkled on the soil. I grow to become undone, to lose what never belonged to me. My roses are black and infinite, my thorns delightful. I stopped drinking love and now I am intoxicated with the wine overflowing in my heart. Taste it and be one again, flawless, forgotten, expired from dead desires wrenching in your puppy heart.

First Infinity

Words spoken from love like water find their way into the heart and kiss a forgotten law to life. But in the ocean of silence, words mean nothing and fall outside the known. No thought or word describes me. No feeling or hand can touch me.

I am your best friend, your dream. I am your wealth, your longing, your dream of freedom.

You can't draw my face or remember any of my names. Yet you are me eternally, anointed by my breath, my second by infinity.

Enormous Beauty

I am lucky to spend the rest of my life with me. Every day—every minute, every second—I get to be with me! If anyone has any quarrels with me, it's because they don't know of my divinity—or their own. If they knew their nature, nothing could give them a reason to complain, and if they complain because of ignorance, I smile because I know so dearly who I am, because I know so dearly who they are. Such is the enormous beauty here.

In You

It's not within my power to love you more, or less. I am helpless in loving what you are. I have mapped your soul with mine. I know your light, your joy. I know your darkness, the secrets you managed to keep even from yourself. You don't know it yet, but we are one. You are my love and my love is free and limitless in you.

Through Darkness

A black cat walking like a lion through the garden of my ignorance. I close my eyes, open them again. The black fur is gone. Only the lion lingers in the shadows. Look, I am not this lion. I am not that cat. I am the one they walk through. The one they will remember in their dreams. The one they smell through darkness.

Is

It doesn't get better than this. This moment, and then the next. It doesn't get better than this. Now, and now, *perpetuus*. Not because it's good, not because it's special but because it is complete—in the sense that nothing else exists. This is it. This. Only this. Is. Now. Nothing else. Ever. Not before. Not later. This. Now: Dog. Sunshine. Water. Tree. This. Is. Is. Is. Is.

Any Speaker

My roots stretch into space where the silence is dark, blue, and speckled with stars. I am spinning, creating webs of meaning; illusory, momentary. My roots sustain the Earth, by chance. When the body is nothing, I am still all. The creation is mysterious and meaningless yet alluring in its loving evolution. Because at the end of words, worlds remain; fresh, true, and free of any speaker.

Trembling

While the sun is in the sky I mend the torn clouds. Under the moon lamp I read holy books about myself. Someone (Ryokan) taught me how to breathe while I was in the womb. Now I gasp every time I read him. His face is mirrored in the puddles. The rains have started, the sun is afraid and trembling.

It

Truth is either a long poem or a very short one. There are either many footnotes or none at all. There are either numberless syllables or a single one. It's either difficult to pronounce or effortless. When you speak of me, I am your words. When I speak of you, you are the content of each word. It doesn't matter if I mumble or stutter: this is it. It doesn't matter if I'm smart or stupid: *this* is. I pronounce you. I don't write your outlines; I build you as I speak. I am your creation; this is it. *This*.

Really Is

This grainy moment frees itself from the grip of memory and anticipation. This grainy moment is all I have. It's beautiful in its harshness. Blinding light forces me to see what is. It's both tender and brutal. It's not what I think about it, not what I wish from it, but what this moment really, really. Is.

Many Times

Nothing is known. Nothing is given—except your body and a world to put it in. Nothing is gained; you have to leave it all behind. Yet you live as if you own your thoughts, as if you own the space you occupy. Every hope must die, I'm sad to say. Every dream must crash against the shore, every safety net be ripped asunder. As long as I hold on to reefs, I suffer. Almost there. I have believed it true so many times.

The Wind

With the eyes of memory I don't see myself anymore. I see the vastness of what contains my mind. There is not a feeling I haven't felt, not a thought I haven't thought, not an experience I haven't had. Yet it's all gone. I remember myself as I am, as I openly scatter life into the wind.

Wind Undone

Plugged in, amplified, intensified, expanded, released, diminished, evaporated, exhaled into the void. Gone, gone, gone, lost in the wind, undone.

At Yourself

So completely at the mercy of God. Vertigo. Nothing is in my power. Was it really necessary to take out the knife? I would have listened anyway. You stole my attention and diverted it at the same time. The first time the knife was aimed at me. The second time the knife was aimed at you. How could I bear it? I will take the knife a thousand times. Don't aim it at yourself.

A Given

What is love? Can anyone tell me in a single word? Is there a love without expectation or demand? And can anyone tell me how love is lost? Could it ever disappear? Now I love you, now I don't—what was it really that you loved, what was it that you lost? Does love come with conditions or is it free? If there are conditions, is it love? What is the responsibility of love? How to give what others need and how to receive what's given? Can you find that open space that enfolds anyone who enters? Can you see how love is not a gift, that it is a given?

Be Smiled

This morning the light passes right through me. It illumines everything in me that was hidden, forgotten, or denied. This morning the light passes right through me. I am that place where nightfall never comes. This morning the light passes right through me. I am that place where darkness dries up and breaks into a million pieces; darkness turned into dust and I am nothing, only light, a kiss waiting to be kissed, a smile waiting to be smiled.

Always Was

And yet love is flooding every area so deeply and everything is washed away. Nothing remains of what was known. It's the type of love that melts the heart and reinvents the world. The love that can't be called love, amour, amor. The love that doesn't have a name. The love that lost its limitations, the love that never dies. The love that finally was known for what it always was.

Of Yourself

Yellow petals creating beauty, life's ephemeral dream, life and death in endless cycles and beyond that, beyond that which is always present, always welcoming with love, always remembering who you are, always forgiving what you thought was unforgivable. And on it goes out into the unknown where the only known is who you are, what you last remembered of yourself.

For Sure

This is so completely insane that it must be true. This is so completely silent that my brain explodes from the noise. This is so completely beautiful that it's undeniably ugly. In a whiplash I am, in a whiplash I am no more. A reality fairytale, for sure.

But Love

Too lazy for words. Too lazy for anything but love. Too lazy to be right. Too lazy to be wrong. Too lazy to experience anything but being. Too lazy to act without presence. Too lazy to be distracted and deluded. Too lazy to be appropriate. Too lazy to despair. I have no time for detours. Too lazy for anything but love.

I'm Going

I can't report on what is happening now. An internal laughter spreading, bubbling up from remote areas of this body. Underground volcanoes, newly discovered planets. I can't identify myself as per usual. My hand is not more mine than yours. The mystery lives through these eyes, yours and mine. It's not for me to know the how, the when, the what—of anything. I am eaten whole. There is nothing left of me. Such a relief to not know the way at all. Such a relief to be completely lost. To not know from where I came or where I'm going.

Ho Ho (Epilogue)

I went bananas, I went ballistic, I went all the way, I went beatific. A quiet explosion and good bye, farewell to God. I love you. Be thy will. Whatever. I am done. Peak a boo! Ho, ho, ho!

Acknowledgments

Thank you, Rosemi Mederos, my awesome editor. It's always a joy to work with you. What's next?

And thank you *l i f e* for hosting me.

Charlotte Brady has previously published two books of poems and a novel in Swedish. *The Last Star* is her third book in English and the third book in the trilogy, The Golden Passage. Her poetry explores the mystery of life and the search for freedom. After living in Sweden, New York, Jamaica, and Barbados, she has now settled in Miami where she lives with her family. Blending essential oils and making fragrances is her favorite pastime.

www.charlottebrady.com

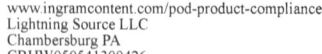

www.ingramcontent.com/pod-product-compliance
Lightning Source LLC
Chambersburg PA
CBHW050541300426
44113CB00012B/2209